# THE SOURLANDS

## BOOKS BY JANA HARRIS

### Poetry

*Pin Money*
*The Clackamas*
*Manhattan as a Second Language*
*The Sourlands*

### Novel

*Alaska*

### Chapbooks

*This House That Rocks with Every Truck
    on the Road* (poems)
*The Book of Common People* (poems)
*Who's That Pushy Bitch* (poems)
*Family Matters* (fiction)

### Poems Adapted for the Stage

*Fair Sex* (a play by Lynn Middleton
    based on poetry by Jana Harris)

# The
# SOURLANDS

## Poems by
## JANA HARRIS

*Ontario Review Press / Princeton*

Grateful acknowledgment is made to the following journals, where many of these poems first appeared, sometimes in a slightly altered form: *Ahnoi!, Calyx, Fine Madness, Gargoyle, Michigan Quarterly Review, Ms. Magazine, Ontario Review, Permafrost, Plainswoman, Room, The Seattle Review.* "Going Home Alone" was first published as a broadside by the San Francisco State University Poetry Center and Jungle Garden Press; and was incorporated into a sculpture by Carl Dern, titled "Medicine Bundle." "On the State of Housewifery in Jersey" was included in *Fair Sex*, a play by Lynn Middleton based on poetry by Jana Harris, premiered at the 18th Street Playhouse, NYC, 1984.

The author would like to thank Raymond Smith, Alicia Ostriker, Kathy Ellingson, and Mary Mackey for their editorial help; Mark Bothwell and Marie Dern for their many readings of these poems; and Joyce Carol Oates for her support and inspiration.

Cover Design: JC Oates

Publication of this book was made possible in part by a grant from the National Endowment for the Arts.

**Library of Congress Cataloging-in-Publication Data**

Harris, Jana.
    The Sourlands : poems / by Jana Harris.
        p.    cm. — (Ontario Review Press poetry series)
    ISBN 0-86538-068-6
    I. Title. II. Series.
PS3558.A6462S68 1989
811'.54—dc20                                    89-33949
                                             CIP

Typesetting by Backes Graphic Productions
Printed by Princeton University Press

ONTARIO REVIEW PRESS
in association with Persea Books

Distributed by George Braziller, Inc.
60 Madison Ave., New York, NY 10010

For the steadfast and true:
Leigh Bienen, Lorna C. Mack, Cindy Derway

# CONTENTS

# SHIPWRECKED IN USELESS BAY

# On Sunday, Blind Rain

the Lantern Inn
breakfast,
at the round table
seed farmers play
a game with dice
order biscuits'n gravy

in the corner
Blind Rain eats
pancakes
his eyes, slits
in his shaved
gray head,
his voice repeats
wavers
singing in Swinomish
to the throw
of the dice
*eeh yah yah eyee*

Mom, the only woman
playing, wins

a tourist lady
looking for antiques
asks Blind Rain
to sing it again

the gamblers brace
themselves
the waitress
freshens their coffee
on the house, she says

the tourist lady
sits down with Blind Rain

the dice louder now
and angry

  *eeh yah yah eyee*

  *at Mukilteo*
  *the white man came*
  *they say, Indians*
  *were there, they say*
  *Swinomish, Tulalips,*
  *they say*

a gambler throws
the dice, Mom sighs,
Blind Rain laughs,
slaps his knee

  *Diggers even were there*
  *they say*

"Diggers," Blind Rain
shakes his head
at the air

  *everyone wore jackets*
  *with long tails on,*
  *they say Hummingbird*
  *flew down to see*
  *white men dressed*
  *in raven clothes*

  *they called it*
  *Treaty Day, they say*

*Chief Ed Joe beat a drum*
*with the moon's face*
*inside, they say*

a dairyman rattles
the dice cup, throws
to the tune of Blind Rain

*they sang this in*
*the smokehouse, they say*

the tourist lady
goes back to Kirkland
with Chief Ed Joe's
smokehouse song which
Blind Rain warns her
not to steal

in the corner
Blind Rain eats
pancakes
syrup, a yellow mountain
of butter, chanting
to the rattle
of the dice cup

I'm the only one left
he says, when I'm gone
this song won't
sing no more

*eeh yah yah eyee*

# What Saved Him That Night

the *Bellybiters?*
you don't want to know
a thing about them,
on your way
to work one morning
on Reservation Road
a lone figure
in headdress
a walking staff,
don't look, just
drive on by
his face
cannot be seen,
a cult, you say
devil worshipers,
but down on
Pull and Be Damned Road
it says: Church
of the Nazarene,
drunken inbred Indians
you think, but
that's how smart they are
descendants of the raven
and the loon
no one knows their names,
this high school boy?
he had hummingbirds
for eyes,
he molested
a little tribal girl,
they came through
his bedroom window
one night, took him

behind the curtain,
poked him with sticks
at first, finally
his lungs filled
with voices
of his ancestors,
he sang their songs,
a language
he had never heard,
that's what saved him
that night
otherwise, white men
would have found him,
his stomach eaten
as if by sharks,
but after that
this boy
was never right,
the hummingbirds
were gone
from his eyes,
he went hunting
one day, he
put the rifle
to his head,
just a bunch
of Indians drinking
playing the bone game
you think, but
you wouldn't want them
coming in your window
one night, you
would never survive
their torture,
even if you were filled
with the spirit

of your ancestors
you would still
be lost, you
are not a descendant
of the raven
and the loon, there
are no hummingbirds
in your eyes,
the spirit
of your ancestors
never learned to sing

# The Gospel
# According to Rudy Coldmountain

a while back, two cops
come looking for a haystack burner,
they find us on the beach
burning old clothes,
caulking boats with rags,
they find the noise of waves
confusing, they complain
our town is full of dogs
running crazy as sockeye when
we make magic on a spawning creek,
these cops look at us and see
something stuck crosswise in a box,
when we meet their eye
they look away, shuffle
their feet as children do
so they will not hear thunder
and be afraid, they ask
about the haystack burner,
we say we don't do such things,
they ask: whose boat is this?
we tell them: Raven's
just then the dogs catch a rat, shake it
fling it away, a sign
we tell them: *take care*
*the tide is not boiling*
*where you put your boat in the water,*
*waves pulling people under is dangerous,*
*it rains hard, clears up,*
*but always rains again,*

these cops look at us as if
to pass our hands through fire
for offending the weather,
they ask: when will you think over
this way of life? we tell them:

when the ravens turn white

# This House of Breath

We watched the tide begin to slack
the minus tide got smaller,
bad things happened:
our boats grew waterlogged and sank
our firewood turned black
without burning,
when our axes rebounded
we became suspect,
then our knives failed to cut,
everyone said: "we'll pay you after fishing,"
but the herring grew white spots
getting old in the slough,
when the ocean stole our possessions
when we were crowded
out of our house by water
we knew, even our dogs
snapped their eyes at us

We went up the mountain,
each rock in the road sang:
bring the hammers, bring the pots,
leave the herring rake,
we carried clams in a bucket
we carried rifles,
ladders one at a time,
we carried more
than we could manage, dropping some
pressing the rest to our chests,
we found another house

We put rags in the broken window
rags up the rat hole,
we placed our knives and forks

upright in a can,
at first we thought: like a loon
we have shaken ourselves free of water
but here it drips off our eaves
in a steady stream,
a house that leaks makes
the sound of people weeping

We sharpened our axe
with a file, our knife
on a bluestone,
our dogs sharpened their teeth
on an elk bone,
we put on woodpecker hats
flapped our arms
folded our arms
still, at night we double over with cold,
remembering the way a herring jumps,
the way its tail
even on a cloudy day
reflects the light

# Watching Geese on Fir Island Road

you can't know how empty it is now
this red tulip field, there in the shadow
of the dike a thousand white geese their wings
tipped in ink, to hear them: such chatter

like schoolchildren, you watch from your cars,
separate, some of you with cameras,
binoculars, so busy these birds,
you think: we have never been as intimate

as geese, we don't even speak to one another,
when suddenly they rise: a white robe
beyond the dike to the sea, north, a nation
of birds, you have never felt so unimportant,

these birds might be your children leaving
the room you papered with bright flowers rows
of them, you stand on the roadside searching
your pockets, something is missing there, how

can a tulip field that red be silent?

# After Reading Marguerite Duras
# We Celebrate Electricity

Our Shed on First Street,
Useless Bay

you would think it was Paris, the end
of the occupation, you would think that's what
electricity meant here, lifting the blackness,
the end of the woodstove, the camp furnace
leaking gas thrown out, plug in the hot plate,
refrigerator, with endless hot water
we scrub black from our fingernails,
we are repatriated, our faces no longer
distorted by camp light, we are called
back from the dead, François has found us,
snuck us out disguised as what we almost were,
corpses, though we still find ourselves by habit
doing the old things: heating water by fire,
cooking in the dark, rationing a cup of hot water
for dishes, we still bring in the cold box
before it freezes, everything black, the pot
bottoms, the pail to heat water,
when we close our eyes against the electric,
we remember the way flame licks
the side of a lamp, we forget for a moment
that Berlin has fallen, gone the soot
black hair, our books, papers buried in ash
as if under rubble, you would think that
was what electricity meant here,
the end of a war, secrets to unlearn,
the neighbors had no idea what went on here,
at night we still hear them: Germans
slinging guns over their shoulders,
but it's the end, in the distance
the last snipers on the rooftops, it's over,
everywhere girls in clean dresses
dancing with soldiers recently home

# Just a Girl

Brunette bob, all legs,
I call her *Vogue Model*
she says she is
taller than any other
third grader in the world

In a too short pink dress,
knees dotted with goose flesh,
she pumps the pedals
of the pink bike,
a white plastic basket
strapped to the handlebars

Skidding to a stop,
hoisting herself
onto the bow
of a battered blue boat,
her shorter *compadres* follow,
she gives orders
and is obeyed

After the smallest
walks the plank
they wait for Benjy,
a dwarf boy who
stops by the woodpile
calling to the crew
of Battered Blue:
"don't you beat me
with that board"

Quick as fire
she is "man overboard,"
two-by-four in hand

aimed dead center
for Benjy who does not
run, but halts,
"don't you, don't you . . ."
repeated like a chant,
a cheer from the high school
football game
three blocks away

Her *compadres* stand
on the sidelines,
shining stones, their eyes
wet with passion,
the dwarf boy
is all head
a dent in his
high blond brow,
the Vogue Model brings
the board's butt-end
closer to the space
between his eyes

Even the neighbor's collie
comes out to watch
the tortured look
on Benjy's face:
"if you do
I'll tell on you,"
the Vogue Model drops
her weapon,
"who'd believe you?"
says the tallest
third grader in the world,
"I'm just a girl"

Just a girl
in a too short pink dress
with a pink bike,
a white plastic basket
strapped to the handlebars,
just a girl
commands her *compadres*
to reboard Battered Blue
as Benjy
retreats towards home

The tallest third grader
in the world stands
on the bow, a wind
billowing her dress
up into her face,
goose flesh rising
on her knees,
in anger she beats
down her skirt,
holding it fixed
between her thighs

The collie dog and I
walk into the street
to reproach her,
she is all sweet smile
turning a pink cheek
she speaks in words
so well rehearsed

*I'm just a girl*

## Civic Duties:
## *My Neighbor, Arny*
## *Volunteer Fireman*

If there's a fire over on the Reservation
and the next day you don't ask Arny,
"where was the fire?"
he'll sulk, lie on his disintegrating couch
in front of the TV, his five-pound dog
Muffin perched on his stomach the size
of a woman seven months gone.

Arny takes Muffin and Muffin's box
to work with him over on the Res
where he builds houses
the government gives the Indians
to make sure they'll never stand
on their own two feet.

                    If you don't ask,
"where was the fire?"
he'll snap his red suspenders, spit into his
spit jar, and not even show any interest
in MASH as snow from the couch
cushions turns his hair to white.

But if you rush out of the house when
Arny pulls up in his two-toned red and black
pickup, ask with all the enthusiasm
you can muster, "Arny,
where was the fire last night?"
he'll say, "come in for a rum 'n Coke,"
and you'll hear all about it while staring
at Arny's favorite jigsaw puzzles
framed on the wall.

             You'll admire one
of the pistols mounted above the TV,
he'll tell you it's an Avon bottle,
you thought it was a gun because
of the rifles roosting in the armchair,
the three-barreled *web foot*
Arny is making from a kit strewn
over the coffee table. You'll wonder
where the bullets go, but forget to ask.

"Ol' Rough Raven was doin' a Power Dance,"
says Arny pouring you a drink
in a *Coke Is It* glass.
"Said he was standin' up, but
he was hands and knees
on the kitchen floor. I don't know what
a Power Dance is, but the flame
on Raven's roof went like this":
he sways moving his feet in
rapid little steps, sliding steps,
making different fast movements
in time to the TV, jerking his head
out of beat. "In celebration," says Arny
his mouth puckered in bad feeling,
"of setting another house free."

# Sue Ellen

the Indians who cannot find
their way from the waterfront
tavern to Jo's on Mill Road
pick her yard to sleep in, because

it looks like no one lives there,
she watches the sleeping Indians,
searches the shopping news
for bargains, she sits in one

of the two chairs, one feeble, one with
so many coats of paint she
doesn't know what color it is,
she is getting better and better

at taking five quarters to the Mercantile
to buy dinner, this week
the bargain is frozen pizza,
dinner for eighty-nine cents is

the best she can hope for, the change
not enough to pay bills—a postage
stamp never meant that much before,
she cooks frozen pizza on top

of the furnace which takes wood and more
wood and will not give heat, the camp
stove, the little propane tank, the one
light bulb plugged into the neighbor's

garage, the floor could use
a good sweeping but in an hour
no one would know, the toilet is
the exciting thing and she can

stand in the new shower
pouring buckets of water heated
on the stove over her head,
everyone agrees skylights

give her house an artistic touch,
the skylights leak
even when it's not raining, still
it's hard to believe

it was a chicken coop before
she moved it away from the big house
the one she regrets selling
to a man with sons who drive by her

on the street screaming names,
at night the neighbor's porch light
lights the bathroom, it's hard
to see the clothes there hanging

from nails, she has cold running water,
washing dishes in cold running water
has done her hands good, but
the pots are greasy and like everything

else covered with soot, if she doesn't
remember to bring the cold box
in after dark the milk will freeze,
some nights the sponge freezes

in the sink, at sundown she goes
to the laundromat, it's warm there,
light to read by, a sink to wash
the soot from her hair, men

from the boats at the laundromat
night after night dismiss her
as a woman who has hair and a lot
of clothes to wash, she wonders

why they come here to get stoned,
remembers the danger of water,
she goes home alone, sleeps
under the eaves, smoke from the woodstove

gives her hay fever, but it's warm
there, for breakfast she eats leftover
pizza, watches the sleeping
Indians stir at first light,

if she had coffee, she thinks
she would offer them coffee,
when the eight o'clock whistle blows
they leave the same way they came,

slowly and without a word

# Arny Yells from His Front Porch, MERRY CHRISTMAS

I run outside with a bottle of Old Crow,
he complains that he can't train people's asses
to leave him alone over the holidays,
today he makes pickled herring
cutting bald onions, he says two dollars
is a lot to pay for a pound of dead fish,
adds sugar, vinegar, cloves boiling
on the stove of the tattered house he grew up in,
the sink where his father died doing dishes
filled with canning jars, black plastic
over the windows so no one will know he's home,
Arny's dog Muffin watches us and TV wrestling,
Arny's New Year's resolution is to put Muffin
in neutral, her broken leg heals by itself
the vet says *kick her*, if she squeals it's mending
the way it's supposed to, Arny says
his problem is he's so damn bored,
on Christmas night we eat pickled fish
studying his photo album, all the bear
he's shot, all the boats he's fished from,
every barren island in the Aleutians,
when we come to his girlfriends,
I ask: who's that man in the picture
with Bambie? he says, a rich guy from Texas,
if her husband caught her, he'd shoot 'em both,
he says for Bambie he would have fixed up
this house, this room painted old rose,
a strange color for a bachelor even with a patina
of stove oil, Arny says his mother painted it
pink before she jumped ship in 1944
when his mother's boyfriend and his father

settled things one Christmas right in this room,
his father stayed with the kids and died
of heart failure doing dishes, Arny says
Bambie is the closest he's come
to painting these walls, he kicks Muffin,
Muffin squeals, Arny says: I'll never
be a father if I put that dog in neutral

# Melody of the Beasts

so ugly she could break
daylight with a stick,
that's what the men said
when she went into town

(fell face forward on
a stoveburner, four-foot-ten,
the lenses of her glasses
thick as she was tall)

with talk like that Melody
stayed home with her cows
which she watched over
day and night, wore herself out

feeling so much obliged
to everyone and every
task, and still Dazzle Girl's
calf smothered at birth,

"tried too hard and prayed
too little," she said turning
the next cow back to God
who couldn't do worse, but

the hour of Melody's
best friend's funeral was
the hour that heifer
went into labor,

"Sue Cora, I'm going
to miss your last service,"
Melody heard her
best friend laugh, that was

when the animals
began to oblige her,
Flicka's Fox tried
all morning to skip

the birth by stealing
another's calf,
*How dare anyone*
*call them dumb beasts,*

Melody sang
—so ugly she could break
daylight with a stick,
the men said when

she went into town

# Waiting for the Broodmare

all night you listen to the banging of her feed bin,
hooves shuffling through straw,

she keeps the moon in orbit, holding fast,
her gravity, her pull determined, she drips milk

chews hay, you are all coffee nerves, slit-eyed,
sleep deprived, Monday she senses a chill,

Tuesday wisps of cloud put her off,
Wednesday frost, Thursday a suspicious presence

in the barn somewhere, Friday you are
so exhausted from this sleepless vigil

you cannot read her, she sees it in your face,
waits you out, her stomach pendulous, on her

side asleep you watch this watery planet's moon
*passage* and *piaffe*, she groans, legs outstretched

rigored, eleven months in orbit, you have been
sleeping in the barn for weeks, the milk

drips wax onto her thighs, at four a.m.
she lies down, strains, gets up, eats,

from outside the stall, you see her heart beat
hear her old house skeleton shift, imagine how

the moon swims the canal, forelegs first, diving
onto the straw-clay floor of your life

# What the End Was Like

*for Grace Paley*

i.
this is what you think you remember:

an overcast afternoon in early spring
when you were bringing the horses
in from Mountain Meadow, too much
new grass could bring on colic,
buttercup, a case of scours,
the timothy and fescue
broken only by broom in yellow bud,
at the pond, still-green cattails and snow
geese like loaves of baking bread, below
the plateau, blue spruce rolled into islands
of the Strait of Juan de Fuca and water
so calm it was impossible to think
this was the Pacific

his ear cocked to the danger
of bee drone, you haltered the big palomino,
pulling him toward the barn,
the others took note, chewed faster,
splinters of green falling
from their mouths, the geese
gathered in discussion as metal horseshoe
clank sparked orange against the trail stones

ii.
all your life you had been
preparing, though That Day came
so suddenly not an animal

cocked an ear nor the pond
moved a wrinkle to announce
the enormous noise and streaking
gray, that needle-nosed barracuda
overhead so close you could read white
numbers beginning with the letter N----

later you recalled the fourth grade:
diving beneath a metal desk
you saved yourself from falling walls
in an earthquake drill, but
the great noise came upon you
quicker than that,
quicker than any schoolyard
*ashes, ashes, we all fall down,* coming
with such suddenness the horses didn't
have time to shy nor the snow geese take
to water, the white birds' wings
splayed against the beach as if mown down,
each horse plummeting to the ground
leaving you holding a slackened cotton rope

somewhere in each animal cell
a genetic message screamed:
"when you hear this noise
fall like the stone you will become,"
a gene lost to you the only thing
upright except the spruce and blue-
green horizon into which the great noise
moved like a dart to the Naval Air Station,
lost, off course, you presume,
vanishing as suddenly as it came
without even time to consider:
there's no place to hide

the geese, gathering their wings, rose up,
the horses like fallen leaves dotting
the field, the palomino lying beside you
in the stone-strewn trail, all the birds and horses
rose up, shook the dust of the end
of the world from their undersides,
bowed their heads and ate

# Mushroom Hunting with Maxine

Cascade National Forest, dirt road
off to the right, ruts so deep they
are year-round water holes, dead-
ending at granite-wall cliffs

Of a gravel pit, parking lot
for trucks and dirt-bike trailers,
go-carts, three-wheelers
roaring up the sheer north face as
riflemen target an abandoned De Soto,
the noise and exhaust worse
than a New York City street, we
—four poets and a scientist—
brace ourselves as if to walk
up West 14th and Broadway

Gathering bags of oysters
unhinged from fallen logs, fingering
the white canvas of a board-hard conk
Maxine instructs: most anything growing
from wood decay is edible,
pink is okay, watch that red coral, white
tastes like cold shredded chicken salad

The trailbikers, children
too young to drive and helmetless,
rev their twin-cylinders beneath
bullet-riddled Smokey the Bear
*Only You Can Prevent Forest Fires*
posted on every tree, though anything
with four legs or wings has fled this place,

leaving only the rubble of clear-cut
trees and second growth,
Maxine points out a dreaded amanita
as biker faces exclaim: mushrooms?
store-bought only, please,
an on-the-side for nothing but
steak more expensive an ounce
than the hourly minimum wage

Under silver-dollar-leafed salal
and saw-toothed Oregon grape, *gold*
we yelled so loud you'd think that's what
we found, gilled and ruffle-skirted,
a chanterelle beside an old logging road
near the dinosaur remains
of turn-of-the-century cedars forced
year after year to witness
shooting mishaps and, once in a while,
a terrible dirt-bike accident

We tramp upcreek through sphagnum past
hardwood maple wreckage into what was
once chanterelle hunting ground,
as if the loggers knew
how to get rid of mushroom lovers
(those non-eaters of meat and conservers
of trail-bike fuel who would have handguns
taken away from everyone), the noise
of rifles and dirt bikes so loud
not one birdvoice squeaks through

None of us has ever seen
a giant purple boletus,
we ask Maxine: will I die, if I . . . ?
unsure, she nibbles (see,
you can peel off the skin),
our bags full, we decide against
parboiling to remove its hot-pepper taste,
heads heavy with noise,
we walk toward home

Praising the silence of fungi

# THE BAD DAUGHTER POEMS

# Going Home Alone

like a face she remembers
the front window,
front door, in the yard
cordwood stacked ten by ten,
a three-legged sawhorse
grazing by the Gravenstein,
like brush fires she remembers
the copper windfalls, rolling
through the buckthorn,
through the sapling fence
taller than the house now
taller than the cookstove pipe
where woodsmoke rose
blue as the front stoop spruce,
the door—open
and funnel-mouthed—
inside rain talking
on the tin roof, talking
to her pokeberry-dyed blouse
in the closet left behind,
talking to the ghost
of a woman making the bed
the noise of sheets
flying across the mattress
free-standing for a moment
their ghost shadow
blocking the window
blocking the copper windfall
candles which lit her days
which burned her path
to that bed
which have brought her
back again and
again

# The China Boy Horse

Down the arroyo
she rides the China Boy horse
through the buckeye trees
across Rancho San Felipe del Rey
across the brown hills
down to where she smells
spring on Cow Withers Trail.
Pulling the bay horse
tight on the bit
sucking her stomach
she breathes the March air,
remembering

*Only that morning*
*their solemn voices had told her,*
*a girl the age*
*when a horse was a danger*
*breaking her bones*
*breaking something inside her*
*a woman, a woman, they'd called her*
*and she . . .*

Into the arroyo-shade
presses the China Boy horse
tail black as tarweed
neck the color of clay dirt.
Sucking the smell
of manzanita and madrone,
her stomach tight as the reins
tight as her arm
in line straight to the bit.
But then in the buckeye thicket

and chaparral
a manstranger spying
as she rides down the trail.
Digging her bootheel
into horse-flesh-rib
cracking a willow quirt
over his flank,
she gallops across
the cow-terraced hills,
behind her the manstranger
following, running on foot.
Faster she presses the China Boy horse
through the dead Spaniard's orchard
through bayleaf smell and bluejay squawk,
faster the manstranger
running behind her
through red clay dust
through

*Only that morning*
*their solemn voices had told her,*
*a girl the age*
*when a horse was a danger . . .*

Faster the hooves,
the bay gelding's tail
like her hair raised
in the wind of their gallop.
Then smelling spring
she pulls tight on the reins,
the man, chest heaving
stationary in the gully below,
one hand in the waist of his pants
motioning up to her, moving
his lips into the shape of

*Only that morning*
*their solemn voices had told her . . .*

Turning the head
of the China Boy horse,
serpentining down
the cow-terraced hill
she aims the bay gelding
dead center
at the manstranger's smile,
aims hooves that beat the red dirt
that echo like bullets
through the dead Spaniard's orchard.
The stranger, moving
at the crack of a bone,
his lips in the red dust
as he falls beneath
hooves beating louder
hooves beating louder than

*Only that morning . . .*

## Y Las Tres Chicas de Yelapa

In the morning
behind Margarito
and the horses for hire
*las tres chicas*
climb down the trail
from the pueblo
heads balancing enameled pots
selling their mama's pies
to *turistas*
who come on the boats
"buy, buy
*coco, limon.*"

Going among the *Federales*
waiting for someone,
come ashore from an armed PT boat
their machetes, their *pistolas*,
their rifles cocked under one arm
"buy, buy
*coco, limon.*"

*Las tres chicas*
with their plastic bags full of change
each in a skimpy dress
and not even seven
roll their eyes seductively
*"yo no sé nada, señores,"*
dividing out the pesos faster
than *Americanos* with pocket computers.

Going among the *turistas*
in the *Cafe de la Playa*
who talk of world affairs,
sex clinics, and Carlos Castaneda.

Going among the dogs and donkeys
who fight over garbage
and coconuts strewn across
the beach
empty of grenadine
and *coco-loco* liqueur

"buy, buy
*coco, limon,*
no change
*no comprendo,"*
speaking to each other in English
better than anyone could know.

Going past the bay
of bright fish swimming
as shadows grow across the palm mountains,
*y las tres chicas*
follow Margarito and the horses
up the steep trail
to the pueblo
back to their *cabañas*
decorated in laundry,
back to *sus madres*
soaking the corn and grating the cocos.

Watching the *Federales*
their rifles and money sacks
on the tables of the cafe below,
watching the *Federales* waiting
for someone,
*las tres chicas:*
"*Ola, ola,* Coca-Cola
Mobil Oil *con su 'boata,'"*
counting their plastic
sacks full of change.

# On the State of Housewifery in Jersey

*Pray for us, O Holy Mother of God:*

    *In the name of the Father*
she melts winter-frozen kitchen pipes
with a 15-hundred-watt hairdryer
listening to Dr. Crane Ph.D., M.D.'s
Worry Clinic Column read out loud
over the radio:
"The case of Marie M., age 29
a scolding, nagging mother of three"
    *Holy virgin of virgins*
    *Holy mother of Christ*
"follower of equal rights boosters
and the male/female 50-50 fallacy,"
Dr. Crane advising her
on how to prevent "impotent husband"
how to be a one-wife harem
    *Mother of divine grace*
    *Mother most chaste*
when she'd rather be reading
*Love's Tender Fury, Valentina*
—a mere girl when he found her
unconscious in the Connecticut woods—
    *Mother inviolate*
    *Mother undefiled*
or reading the *National Enquirer,*
how to fight boredom
how to avoid catching
diseases from pets.
    *In the name of the Father*
she fights "shelf smog"
I'd rather play tennis decaled
across her company's coming apron,

armed with Spic and Span,
sponges, Pine-Sol, and *Polly's*
*Creative Cleaning Pointers*
   *Lord have mercy*
   *Christ have mercy*
washing off oil-furnace window grime
with toothpaste, and rust
in the shower stall with peanut butter.
Fighting "shelf smog" and primping
in the hall mirror
so those Knights of Columbus
Auxiliary ladies
can't say she's gone to seed
can't say her house
   *Mea maxima culpa*
looks like a cyclone hit it.
Straightening drawers
and sorting closets,
   *Virgin most prudent*
   *Virgin most powerful*
not even noon before
she wants a drink, a Valium
because liquor calories
just go to her hips.
Depressed, remembering back to
   *Queen of angels*
   *Queen of patriarchs*
the diets she's been on:
the Scarsdale rear-end collision diet
the Nine Day Wonder diaper-rash diet
the Mayo Clinic grapefruit
kitchen fire diet.
   *Christ hear us*
as she puts the chicken
cacciatore casserole
on time bake, finding

  *Hail Mary full of grace*
her old tennis balls
in the kids' Little League closet,
thinking that if she could just
  *Blessed is the fruit*
put them in the oven on low heat
Polly says
  *Of thy womb, Jesus*
they'd regain their bounce.

# Waterlemon Bay

St. John, U.S. Virgin Islands
March 28, 1979

i

Carib Sea, she says,
so lovely a face.
Sand the platinum
of Harlow's hair
water, Harlow's eyes
shining up on the bellies
of pelicans flying over
spider-legged people
herding goats
across the conch-covered grave
of Constantina Magdelina,
herding goats with bay rum sticks
thin as their spider arms.
Walking over white coral bones,
she swims beneath ruins
as the men who have come with her
talk of History
of Danish planters clear-cutting
death-apple manchineels
for sugarcane crops.

ii

She is swimming, the men say,
where once there were sugarboats
with slaves and black rats
in their holds,
where once rum-runners
brought mongeese and coconut palms.
Swimming, the men say,

where black rats now sleep above her
in calabash and soursop trees.
History, the men say,
when the mongoose mowed
the sugarcane crops, History
when the hurricane rains
washed the black dirt to the sea.
But as the men watch her swim
they begin yelling warnings of sharks,
calling her back to a land
where rum is cheaper
than a loaf of white bread,
where spider-legged children
suck orange popsicle sticks.

iii

Carib Sea, she says,
so lovely a face.
Sand the platinum
of Harlow's hair
water, Harlow's eyes
shining up on the bellies
of pelicans flying over
as she flies over
the sea creature's sky,
flies over forests
of coral pipe-organ cactus,
the tides, warm as trade winds
blowing through her fingers.

iv

With the water her body moves
though she walks on land
down the man-paved road
past poison-apple manchineels

past spider-legged people
herding goats
across the conch-covered grave
of Constantina Magdelina.
The men tell her news
of an accident
on Three Mile Island
two thousand miles away.
With water she moves
her body rising and falling,
thinking not of their accident
but of parrot fish and flounder
spotted brighter than lipstick.
With the wavecrest she falls
from her bed at night
floating out past the men
waiting for news,
too busy to notice her
riding the crest into the fall.

Above her the jellyfish moon,
what name will they give me,
she wonders—*trumpetmouth
jewfish*—what name for a woman
who had gone to live in the sea?
Easier than walking, she thinks,
easier than lying in bed with a man.
O Carib Sea, she says,
so lovely a face.
It is myself I smell
when I smell of the sea.

# The Scientist's Wife
# Has an Opinion
# On Her Rival

He speaks freely
of their relationship,
he says, we're working
on Helen today,
or, we're not
working on Helen,
she's in the freezer

The scientist's wife
asks, why her?
he says, because
her cells multiply
with astonishing speed

Each night she wonders
if he brings pieces
of Helen home
on his hands,
she is afraid her rival
will take hold
in the mattress,
the kitchen,
move into the house

He is proud, he boasts:
the day after
he put Helen
in the freezer,
he found parts of her
growing
in a neighboring lab

This is what
the scientist's wife
knows about her rival:
she was black
she died
in a state hospital
in the year her husband
was born,
and the cancer
which killed her
lives on, growing
even in a freezer

The scientist's wife
wonders why
no one asks:
what kind of a life
would grow something
that terrible?
in the scientist's wife's
opinion, Helen Lane
has given new meaning
to the meek
who shall inherit
the earth,
that thing which
Helen's womb made
is more powerful
than all of them

Each day her husband
leaves home to study
another woman's parts,
she begs him not to,
someday, she tells him,
you'll bring her
home, I just know it

He shows her
photographs
of Helen's cells
growing,
she tells her husband
he's looking for clues
in all the wrong places,
it's not there,
she says,
the answer

it's not there

# Nameless of the Sourlands

From my window,
grave of the woman
who built my house,
bramble-covered
her name wind-scoured
from the slate, erased
only the words
*who departed this life*
endure

As she endured,
dark, cavern-eyed
I imagine her standing
beside me, a rag-bound foot
on the pine plank floor,
face pressed against
a shuttered pane,
out this window hills
of the fields she tilled

Her hands
a bundle of sticks now
holding memories
of scythe handles, hands
that swung an adz
which hewed oak beams
of a rootcellar, stone
thick and springhouse cold
even in summer, gone now,
only her flatirons
left behind, found
in the privy pit,
what rage, I wonder
threw them there?

Was she heat-crazed
one dog day in August
even her big-bellied hen
panting, the pokeweed
and touch-me-nots
lax-headed, drooping
in the sun, or was she
dreamseeing my life
as I see hers: cutting
years from the red clay
and gray slate fields,
cutting stems
of oxeye daisies left
on the graves of grandmothers
who dug ore from these hills
and coal-fire forged it
into Independence muskets

Could she have foreseen
that though she hand-squared
timbers for this three-story house
there would be,
even in my life, no one
pair of clay-reddened womanhands
writing the laws
of the land her house
was built on?

Could she have known
that still in the Sourlands
a war goes on, that
when I told my neighbors
their dog killed my laying hen,
they sneer-asked, was I
the hillbilly from
Shotgun Corner?
not knowing her name

I could only point next door
where my cabbages
go uncrocked
in her basement,
her kraut recipe
and German name gone
like mine, like the name
of our town taken
in a war not even fought here

Now, above her bald headstone
green corn rolls placidly
up-hill to the sky, and
daughter-like I bring
the flatirons to her grave,
"leave me these," I say,
remnants of a life I have
only begun to imagine,
anger broken and rasping
her windvoice through my walls
scream-searches
for her adz marks on my timbers
for her rusted flatirons,
"leave me these," but
her windvoice steals
my words for the air,
steals the words from
her headstone

From my window,
grave of the woman
who built my house,
bramble-covered,
name wind-scoured
from the slate, erased
only the words
*who departed this life*
endure

# Sending the Mare to Auction

choosing the gelding, younger, more placid,
I remember my mother chose my brother

over me for that reason, today I am
packing my bad girl off to auction,

the whites of her eyes, red, the vet's
hypnotic voice, *temper*, he says, *such*

*a temper*, but her loveliness outweighs
everything, the shape of her head,

the neck arch, I think of Isak Dinesen
leaving Africa—"these horses," she cried

in goodbye—my first mare the one I should
have had as a girl when I was bolder,

one day vicious, indomitable, the next
crying at the gate, already I've forgotten

she bit me with fury, with her hind legs
struck me down, that day I took a crop,

beat her until I could no longer raise
my arm, the look in that mare's eyes said

it made no difference, there was no way to
make this bad girl good, when she struck me

across the face, was that the look my mother
saw in me? lovely thing, the dreams I had

for her, I am shipping her off the way
my mother did me, her black tail flowing

in my dreams, now I wait for the van,
she waits—little clock—by the fence

haunches spread, the stallion watches her
tail cocked, tart, sweating from head to hoof

flesh hot as stove burners, selling this mare
what is it I send to auction?

# The Drought:
# Hands Shelved Above Her Eyes
# She Listens

face hidden from the paint-
blistered porch, from the heat scythe
cutting through the farmhouse door,
gravel road, river of dust
come over the dead field corn, the wind
stronger now in the rattlebox weed
dust coming down the Sourlands like rain
on the garden, skeleton-rowed sunflowers
bent-shouldered at noon and katydids
the only green, poplars sighing
to a cloud-peopled sky, the noise of
chickens, white-hackled, necks bobbing
they stop midswing at the noise of
heat lightning, dry leaves falling and
the sun burning through the other side
of nightfall, hands pressed to her face
eyes hidden from the gravel road
river of dust, rain-lie

# A Dead Cat Story

*for K.*

the Ballad of Aldo & Charlotte
goes like this: for fifteen years
he was her main man

when a veterinarian found
a growth in his abdomen
he filled her with hope, but
when Charlotte ran through her savings
put aside during fifteen years
working as a Kelly girl, hope ran out
and she had to borrow taxi money
to get to the clinic, borrow to put
Aldo down, borrow to have
his tortoise-shell remains turned to ash
and the ash poured into a tall glass-
of-a-gold-papered box resembling
bourbon whiskey at Christmastime

not a dry eye for weeks and
her roommate talked too much,
Charlotte wondered if
her roommate's abrasive chatter
had killed her cat, she couldn't sleep,
she walked the streets wondering
how she could live with a woman whose talk
had killed her main man,
she couldn't work, she wore out
her shoes walking, she got mugged,
her purse, driver's license, journals
of three-years-running, her
Aldo meditations: gone,
she wrote her ex-husband, had he
saved her Aldo letters
thrown away the day they arrived?

her cat and journals sleeping
in dark circles beneath her eyes

she couldn't pay the rent, at age forty,
and without Aldo, she went home
to her mother in Parklawn
to the house her grandfather built
remodeled with a 50's flagstone fireplace
and Astroturf on the sleeping porch,
in Parklawn (as a teenage smart-aleck
she called it "Porkland" and still does)
there were no parks
and no lawns, the only green
the Naval Air Station's camouflaged
B-52 warplanes hovering overhead

in her mother's house
she could not complain about the sulfur-
smelling mill because
it meant her brother went to work,
nor about her mother's two
Persians for whom her only feeling
was contempt

when she heard them scratching
at the screen door, she whispered "Aldo,"
in her dreams his eye,
blinded by surgery into his
metastasized brain, put right

his remains on the window sill,
the gold paper when it caught the light
reminded her: in life
she had been filled and refilled
with hope, but in the end
what was left
was a dead cat

# Bad Daughter Poem

a child, I
remember my mother
waiting on
each word

of her mother's
doctor, the strokes
the delirium, my
memory filled with

walkers, wheelchairs, and
a woman who gave up
tilling the Idaho hills,
a woman I was

not allowed to
call Grandmother
sitting for years
in front of the black

and white Motorola,
at Thanksgiving
rabbit dinner, I
chewed rubber-

band strand, brown
as turkey meat
to the words of a man
I did not call

Grandfather:
"eat the fat, it'll
keep you alive," and
my mother's scolding:

*bad daughter, I*
*was a bad daughter, you'll*
*be sorry, you're*
*a bad daughter too,*

sorry she said she
was sorry, born
a girl, only the two
brothers to hoe potatoes,

bad daughter she was,
she said at her
mother's side through
the insulin shock, the

gangrene, amputations
for years
each night at supper
obsessing over my

Grandmother's illness
until I could taste
the sickbed words
like cauliflower the

high blood sugar, the
paralysis, sauerkraut sting
on my tongue, the blindness:
that's all the fruit

cocktail you get—Sister,
call Billy, Sister,
how's Buster's wife?—
never called by her

given name, my mother
—Sister, remember those

boys eating my winter
apples? those boys, oh

land to Goshen—those
boys who never were there
my mother, hands
wrung so often

they were raw
in my mind, waiting
for her turn and I
watching the maternal

love like money, something
earned, a debt outstanding
to come due with
much interest, never

paid and never paid
*bad daughter, I*
*was a bad daughter, you'll*
*be sorry, you're*

*a bad daughter too,*
a debt named
you-can-be-good-
all-your-life-

and-no-one-will-notice,
passed through the blood
to me, my mother's
account not received

my mother's push,
the try and try and
again try to love
those who will not

give you what
you want, something
in all the wrong ways
I have foreclosed

on the pain flashing
across her brow
as my Grandmother
complained, the ache

in her missing foot
her missing knee,
my mother waiting
for the words

just one of thanks, of
what a good girl,
what a good
and pretty girl,

waiting to be jewel
of those glaucomatous eyes,
and when her mother died
brought home her only

legacy, the worn
nursing home flannel
pajamas, saved
for me, she said:

*bad daughter, I was
a bad daughter, you'll
be sorry, you're
a bad daughter too*

# Now I Lay Me Down to Sleep

Your mother tells you:
at the sanitarium your aunt
fell in love with her doctor,
that's how they knew
she was well enough to go home,
draw back the sheets on your cousin's bed
and find them, white,
hundreds of pinworms,
your mother says: Public Health
insists you be checked in your sleep,
shows you the blood-cherry medicine
which has to turn your mouth
Kool-Aid red and your stomach
inside out to kill worms,
your aunt says: don't
send her to bed without supper,
the golly-awfuls could eat her gut,
bring on colic like Old Blue
in the tarweed pasture
across the street died of last winter,
your mother reminds everyone:
when you were too young to remember,
you ate dirt and horse pucky

That night you say
the *Now I lay me down*,
God Bless your parents,
and take inventory: hard horsehair pillow,
tattered log-cabin quilt made
from the pole-shaped scraps
of your crazy aunt's clothes,
frayed army blanket on top,
gypsumboard walls, unpainted,

nails plastered over in white
flying elephant-shaped clouds,
you hear them before you see
the flashlight's cyclops eye,
your mother giggles,
brushes her shoulder against
your father's white night clothes,
giddy as if drinking champagne
they roll you on your side,
army blanket pulled away, quilt
pulled away, the bottoms of your pajamas
pulled down, elastic stretching
across your stomach like a sling shot,
your mother shows your father how
to hold the light, before you went to bed
you begged them not to—no fair,
two against one—rules you are held to
don't apply here, in your
*Now I lay me down*, you asked God
and even your aunt for help,
your mother guides your father,
flashlight inserted, cold
metal against your skin,
you hear them making
a joke about the birthmark in your cleft,
your prayers for a clean report vanish
as your mother giggles "get that
woolly mammoth," you don't
feel the swat, you're gone
to an elephant cloud
plastered in the wall, then circle
overhead, an angel, the one
you asked to speak to God on your behalf:

*If I should die before I wake,*
*I pray the Lord my soul to take*

# Your Mother

Invites herself to your farm for Christmas
she and your father happen to be
free that day, their real estate agent
busy, no retirement dream-house tours

She gives your husband a copy
of the secondhand army-surplus sweater
you got at sixteen when you wanted
angora or a horse of your own,
*you're* the daughter who entertains,
so you get her styrofoam cup collection
saved from years of motels
and military installations,
you get Yardley soap and red shoes,
to which you remark, "of course
they're not my size," remembering at sixteen
she crammed your foot into a number 5 shoe:
her size, her mother's size (all the women
in the family had to wear the same shoe),
miraculously, when you open the box,
they *are* your size, which your mother insists
she has always worn even before
age swelled her feet, before her mother lost
both legs at the knee, and your larger-than-life
sister came along with number nine feet
which not even your mother could push
into a petite thrift-store Mary Jane,
here you are, age 40, the right size shoe at last
and still as ungrateful as ever

Your mother says she didn't have much time
to Christmas shop between dream-house tours,
when she found an irresistible Chinese chest,
she bought it for herself because
you would have loved it

After brunch they want to watch
your husband ride the horses you've raised,
they've never seen him astride,
they haven't seen you on a horse
since high school, when you demanded
"look at me" every day of their lives,
and your mother complained: horses
raised dust that got her car dirty

You lead Miss Piggy from her stall,
a two-year-old barely broken, nervous
from the moment you separate her
from her feed, her eyes widen to white,
her gravel-truck body shies at your father
walking the roadside, swinging a sack
of beer cans redeemable at three cents apiece

Miss Piggy leaps across the paddock,
her girth slips, the saddle falling beneath her,
you somersault over her pork-barrel flank,
break the fence, collide with a corner post
before your shoulder—a trowel digging in—
strikes the ground, you watch the undersides
of Miss Piggy's white dinner-plate feet
gallop away from you

You can't raise yourself, your leg swells
inside your boot, your mother asks
if you're going to get back on,
someone—your father?—lectures:
a poor football player you'd make,
somehow you limp to the house,
putting ice on your ankle, you look up
Emergency Rooms as your mother
gives you the rest of your Christmas:

When you were born she painted murals
on the wall of their rented house (next door to
the first-in-a-series of dream homes—only
the foundation built on a lot they did not own),
toadstools, frogs, a pig next to your crib,
today she has brought the tattered
worn stencils used all those years ago

Your finger searches for the local
hospital known as Death Valley General,
your husband still outside chasing
the horse you raised from a suckling,
your mother is boxing up Christmas
your father warms the car's engine, leaving
for more dream-house tours tomorrow

Your leg doesn't work the way it did this morning
your father says it's nothing
your mother tells you: when a wall
of their second dream house fell on her,
everyone went right on working as if
nothing happened, this your first memory:
your mother prone and crying,
her leg a side of meat, not unlike your own

Your foot does not meet your ankle the way
it used to, even the arch looks wrong
your mother worries about the danger of X-rays,
when you crawl up to bed, she says
what you need is a hot cup of tea

It's hard coping with everything:
your mother, Christmas,
your first wallpaper, emergency rooms,
something broken in the foot
something broken in the fence
something broken in the heart

## ABOUT THE AUTHOR

Jana Harris has published several books of poetry, including *Manhattan as a Second Language*, and a novel *Alaska*, a Book-of-the-Month Club alternate selection. For six years, she was director of *Writers in Performance*, the literary series of the Manhattan Theatre Club. Presently, she teaches creative writing at the University of Washington and reviews for *The Seattle Times*. Born in San Francisco and raised in the Pacific Northwest, she now lives with her husband in the foothills of the Cascade Mountains, where they raise horses.

ONTARIO REVIEW PRESS
POETRY SERIES

Jana Harris
**The Sourlands**
$9.95 paper

Jon Davis
**Dangerous Amusements**
$8.95 paper

Albert Goldbarth
**Arts & Sciences**
$17.95 cloth/$8.95 paper

Albert Goldbarth
**Original Light**
New & Selected Poems 1973–1983
$12.95 cloth/$7.95 paper

William Heyen, ed.
**The Generation of 2000**
Contemporary American Poets
$14.95 paper

Joyce Carol Oates
**Invisible Woman**
New & Selected Poems 1970–1982
$8.95 paper

Robert Phillips
**Personal Accounts**
New & Selected Poems 1966–1986
$16.95 cloth/$9.95 paper

Order from George Braziller, Inc.
60 Madison Ave., New York, NY 10010